THE MORECAMBE AND WISE JOKEBOOK

The MORECAMBE & WISE Jokebook

by Eric and Ernie

ARTHUR BARKER LIMITED   LONDON

A subsidiary of Weidenfeld (Publishers) Limited

Published in Great Britain by Arthur Barker Limited
91 Clapham High Street
London SW4 7TA

Designed by Joyce Chester

ISBN 0 213 16732 8

Printed in Great Britain by
Butler & Tanner Ltd
Frome and London

Contents

Preface
by Ernie

Do you remember the old song 'My Old Dutch' with its line 'We've been together now for forty years'? Well, that's how long Eric and I have been doing our double act.

Mind you, forty years is a very short time in the history of cross-talk. The double act is as old as theatre itself. As long as we've had entertainers, they've reflected the conflicts of life in their work, exploiting especially the cut and thrust inherent in partnerships, whether between man and wife, father and son or master and servant.

Our grandfathers saw the double act begin to flourish as a separate entity when they took grandma to the Victorian music hall. My grandpa and grandma were quite a double act in themselves!

Then, in the 1920s, when Eric and I were just kids, music hall faded and variety took its place. And it was in the variety theatres of the day that there evolved a legendary crop of cross-talk acts – people like Murray and Mooney, Clapham and Dwyer and the trio of partnerships which was to make up the celebrated Crazy Gang – Nervo and Knox, Flanagan and Allen and Naughton and Gold. And in America meanwhile, acts like Abbott and Costello and Laurel and Hardy were developing the art of the cinema double act.

Before television killed off variety in the 1950s, Eric and I had already established ourselves nationally as cross-talk comics. Since then, through the medium of radio and, later, television we've striven to perfect our act.

People often ask the secret of our togetherness. I'd say it's because we have the same sense of humour – he makes me laugh and I make him laugh. And we've shared the same ambition since we were teenagers – to emulate the cross-talk acts we saw then.

Eric and I would be the first to acknowledge our debt to those who went before us. This book is our tribute to the cross-talk stars (and the jokes) of yester-year.

1 · Introduction

Good evening, ladies and gentlemen and welcome to *The Morecambe and Wise Jokebook*.

Good evening, ladies and gentlemen and welcome to The Morecambe and Wise Jokebook.

Wait a minute – I've just said that!

So that's *where I heard it.*

It gives me great pleasure ...

And it always has.

Do you mind! I'm trying to introduce this book.

Course you are, Ern – go ahead.

A very warm welcome, ladies and gentlemen, to *The Morecambe and Wise Jokebook*. If you'd care to stay with us for the next few pages, we can promise you more laughs than you can shake a stick at and ...

Do you know what the young girl said to the sailor?

No.

That's right!

To continue: Cross-talk humour has been with us since Shakespeare's time ...

Shakespeare? William Shakespeare? I had dinner with him last night.

But Shakespeare's been dead for three hundred years.

I thought he was quiet.

But it was with the introduction of the music hall that ...

You know, I heard something this morning that really opened my eyes.

What was it?

An alarm clock.

Please, Eric, let me introduce this book!

Sorry, Ern, sorry.

... that the art of the double-act began to flower. Consider for a moment ...

Hey, do you know what the young girl said to the sailor?

What again?

That's right!

Consider for a moment the names of those great British music halls: the Empires of Brixton and Hackney, the palaces of variety...

The Houses of Parliament ...

... and those great comedians who graced their stages: Murray and Mooney, Flanagan and Allen ...

Baldwin and Chamberlain. Hey, answer the phone, answer the phone!

But it's not ringing!

Why leave everything till the last minute?

This book, ladies and gentlemen, is our humble tribute to the cross-talk stars of yester-year ...

Hey, you know what the young girl said to the sailor?

We've done that twice already!

That's right! Not to mention Fred Metcalf.

Fred Metcalf?

I thought I told you not to mention him!

Who is he anyway?

Who is he? Only the bloke who helped us compile this book, that's all. And one of the most talented scriptwriters of his generation. And that's not just my opinion.

No?

No – it's his too!

Anyway, on with the book! Enjoy yourselves and we'll see you later.

Hey, Ern, wait a minute!

What now?

Do you know what the young girl said to the sailor?

Look, this is getting ridiculous!

That's right, that's right!

2 · It's a dog's life!

Hey, do you mind, your dog's just eaten my hat!

I don't mind at all. He likes hats.

But it was my best hat!

Well, he wouldn't eat any old hat, would he?

Are you trying to annoy me?

What makes you say that?

It's your attitude.

It's not my 'at 'ee chewed, it's your 'at 'ee chewed.

Anyway, you ought to keep that dog out of here – it's full of fleas.

Did you hear that Isaiah? Don't come in here anymore – it's full of fleas.

Isaiah? Why do you call him Isaiah?

Because one eye's 'igher than the other.

What sort of dog is he, anyway?

He's a Dobermann pinscher. Goes round all day pinching Dobermanns.

Well, you should try and stop him pinching people's hats. And if he doesn't, you should have him put down.

Have him put down? I couldn't do that – he's like one of the family! I'd rather not say which one of the family, mind you. Anyway, I could never get rid of a dog. I'll never forget having our last one put down.

Was he mad?

He was furious! And we'd been such pals. Every day we used to go for a tramp in the woods.

I bet he enjoyed that!

He did. Mind you, the tramp was getting a bit fed up. He was such a clever dog, too. The only dog I ever had that could say its own name.

What was it called?

Woof. You remember the film Lassie Come Home?

Yes.

He was in that.

What part did he play?

The lead. I was in it too, actually – I had a bit part.

What did you do?

I got bit. This dog ran up to me, barking its head off....

But didn't you know, a barking dog never bites?

I did – but the dog didn't. Hickory they called him. What a bad dog.

Why did they call him Hickory?

'Cos he had such a rough bark. One day on the set there was a seat with a notice on it: 'Wet paint.' So he did. I kicked him and he turned into a black-smith.

How do you mean?

He made a bolt for the door.

He sounds worse than old Isaiah here.

There's nothing wrong with Isaiah. He's a lovely dog, aren't you, boy? Last Saturday he took first prize at the cat show.

How was that?

He took the cat.

Didn't you punish him?

I should have done. Trouble is, I spoil him. It works, though. Most of the time I've got him eating out of my leg.

Does he bite you very often?

Not really. Last night, mind you, he gave my leg quite a nasty bite.

Did you put anything on it?

No, he liked it just as it was.

Why is he always biting you?

Well, he doesn't eat meat.

Why not?

Because we don't give him any. We keep him hungry. Makes him a better watch-dog.

A watch-dog? Is he any good?

Well, last week he watched a burglar steal half the house, so you can't say he doesn't do what he's told.

You must be sorry you bought him.

Not really. I bought him because he was unique. And he still is.

How do you mean?

Well, he was the only dog in the pet shop going cheap.

So?

Well, all the other dogs were going 'Woof.'

3 · Flying tonight!

Is this the first time you've been on a plane?

Yes.

Are you nervous?

Me, nervous? Of course not. Hey, look at all those people down there – they look like ants.

They are ants – we haven't taken off yet. You are nervous, aren't you?

Well, just a bit. I mean, what happens if we're five miles up and the engines run out of fuel?

Easy – we just get out and push. Anyway, they know a long time before that something's about to go wrong.

How?

The co-pilot becomes hysterical.

Oh no!

But don't worry about the plane crashing. Remember – in the case of an accident the pilot is always first on the scene.

Oh, I wish I'd gone by ship.

A friend of mine was like you – took the boat instead. Terrible shame.

Why, what happened?

A plane fell on it. Hey, aren't you going to unwrap that chewing-gum before you eat it?

Oh, yes, but why did the air hostess give it to us?

It's supposed to stop your ears popping during the flight.

Does it work?

Sure – it's just a bit difficult getting it out of your ears when you land.

Oh, I'd give anything not to be in this plane at the moment.

Look, take my advice, if you have to fly, much better to go by plane. Anyway, it's only a short journey. We'll be back on the ground again in half an hour.

Half an hour? As long as that?

Don't tell me – you rang up the airport to ask how long the flight took.

That's right.

And the girl said, 'Just a minute.'

Yes.

And you said, 'Thank you,' and put the phone down.

Well, how was I to know? I suppose I'd better ring them up at the other end and tell them I'm going to be late. Can you telephone from an aeroplane?

Everybody *can tell a phone from an aeroplane, can't they?*

No, but how can I get in touch with the people at the other end?

I'm going there – I'll *tell them.*

I wish you'd stop all these jokes. Can't you see I'm very nervous?

You're *nervous? Don't you think I might be scared too? I'm telling you, I get airsick just licking an air mail stamp. Every time I land safely I swear I won't go up in a plane again until they repeal the law of gravity. I hate flying. Hate it. I can't think of a single good reason why the plane should stay in the sky. If something goes wrong, that's it – you've had it. Look, if God had meant us to fly he would have given us wings.*

So why are you flying then?

I have to – I'm the pilot.

4 · This is a mix up!

Excuse me, can you see a policeman round here?

No.

Okay, stick 'em down!

You mean stick 'em *Up*!

Don't confuse me – I'm nervous enough as it is. Just give me your watch.

But it isn't worth anything. It's only value is sentimental.

Let's have it anyway – I feel like a good cry.

You'll feel like a good cry soon when I take you back to the station.

Oh no! Just my luck! Don't tell me I've held up a ...

That's right.

... train driver!

Don't be stupid. I'm talking about the *police* station. I'm a police officer, in plain clothes. You were fooled by this black and white patterned suit I'm wearing.

I ought to have known – it's just a routine check!

Now then, what might your name be?

Well, it might be Cecil – but it isn't.

Well, whatever it is, I'm going to have to ask you to accompany me to the station.

Why? Are you afraid at this time of night?

Just come along quietly if you don't mind.

This could mean promotion for you, y'know. I'm the most wanted man in Workington.

Is there a price on your head?

Yes, but I won't sell. They've offered £1,000 if I'm captured dead.

Yes?

£2,000 if I'm captured alive.

Yes?

And £3,000 if I'm captured dead and alive. And all for one lousy overdue library book!

Really? What's the charge?

16

Tuppence a day.

No – what have they charged you with?

Borrowing with intent. Look, give me a break! What chance have I had? I was born into a criminal family.

How do you mean?

When she had me, my mother had been separated from my father for six months.

What was he doing?

Six months. And I've been following in his finger-prints ever since.

I see what you mean.

I'll never forget my mother's words to me when I first went to jail.

What did she say?

Hello, son.

What were you in for?

Well, I'd started in a small way – picking midgets' pockets.

How could you stoop so low?

Stoop? I was up on tip-toe! I was very young. I can remember it to this day, being hustled into the backdoor of the court with my nappy over my head to avoid the photographers.

What was your mother in jail for?

For something she didn't do.

What didn't she do?

She didn't run fast enough.

Where did they catch her?

In Oxford Street. She'd taken me shopping. I can still see her now, standing by the main door of the shop, with the silver glinting in her hair – and the store detective taking it out, a fork at a time.

And where was your father at the time?

He was dead by then.

What happened to him?

Well, he was on the roof of a paint factory when he slipped, fell through and was drowned in a tank of varnish.

What a horrible way to go.

On the contrary – they say he had a beautiful finish.

Still, I'm very touched by your story. The Super down at the station would kill me if he knew but I'm going to let you go. I'm going to give you one more chance.

Really?

Really. So what have you got to say to that?

Just one thing.

What?

Stick 'em up!

5 · Private eyewash!

Ladies and gentlemen, here is an announcement: The police are looking for a man with one eye ...

Typical police efficiency!

Do you mind! The police are looking for a man with one eye called Lennie.

What's his other eye called?

Please be serious! The police are looking for a man for assaulting women.

Really? I wonder what the pay's like.

Look, this is a serious police investigation ...

I know, I know – you don't have to tell me. I used to be the finest private detective in the land.

You were the finest private detective in the land?

That's very kind of you to say so. Ah, yes, how could I ever forget my first case.

What happened?

I left it on the train between Leeds and Scarborough. How I could have forgotten it, I don't know to this day. But I didn't let it get in the way of my investigations.

Your investigations into what?

Into the Case of the Missing Ring or Who Washed out the Bathtub? I well remember how it started.

Do tell us.

I was sitting at my desk one day – wishing I had a room to go with it – when suddenly a tall girl walked past my window.

How do you know she was tall?

I lived on the sixth floor. Then suddenly the phone rang. Right away I knew something was wrong.

Why?

I didn't have a phone. Then suddenly there was a knock on the doorbell.

A *knock* on the doorbell?

I told you – the ring was missing. And before the day was done, I was on my way to Scarborough. It was a fascinating case. The local police had pronounced themselves baffled. The CID had pronounced themselves 'SID'.

So what did you find when you got there?

I found that a murder had been committed.

A murder had been committed?

I just told you that. I lined up all the suspects except the butler.

Why didn't you line up the butler?

He was the one who'd been murdered. The next day I got up early and grilled them individually for ten minutes.

You did?

Why not? That's the way I like my sausages. Then, after breakfast, I found this bloke in the cellar.

What did you do?

I gave him the third degree. I was relentless. For hour after hour I kept at him, question after question.

Did he confess?

He didn't even answer me.

Why not?

It was the corpse. He had a gun in his hand and a knife in his back. Who d'you think poisoned him?

Who?

Nobody. He'd been strangled.

Who could have done such a terrible thing?

I only knew one thing – the murderer was ruthless.

How was that?

I had Ruth with me.

Did you have any clues?

Not a lot. The wall safe had been opened.

What was in it?

A wall.

Hadn't the thief made any noise?

No, he'd taken things very quietly. But I had my suspicions about one man.

Who?

The cook – a strange bloke with a handle-bar moustache called Tinker.

Tinker? That's a funny name for a handle-bar moustache.

Not really – there was a bell on it.

21

He was your number one suspect.

He was not only my number one suspect. He was my number two and number three suspect.

Why was that?

He'd confessed.

He throttled the butler?

That's right! And my mother had told me never to speak to stranglers.

Did you arrest him?

I tried to but he tried to make a run for it.

Did you run after him?

I did – but he was too fast for me. So I threw away my shirt, then my trousers, then my underpants.

What happened?

Gradually I outstripped him.

Did he put up a fight?

You bet – we went at it hammer and tongs.

Hammer and tongs?

Yes. I won in the end though. I had the hammer.

Well done! And was he found guilty of murder?

He was.

And sentenced to hang?

That's right. But in those days, of course, you couldn't hang a man with a moustache.

No?

No – you had to use a rope.

23

6 · Bottom of the pops!

Would you like to read my new novel? I've got a copy here, hot off the press.

I'd love to – I very much enjoyed your last book. Who wrote it for you?

I'm so glad you liked it. Who read it to you?

No, but seriously, I've nothing but admiration for you as a writer. And I've very little of that.

What you don't seem to realise is that I am, deep down, a very intelligent person. In fact I was just about the most intelligentest person in my school.

So you actually did go to school?

Of course I did. When it came to education my father wanted me to have all the opportunities he never had.

So what did he do?

He sent me to a girl's school.

I bet you gave your teacher a lot of trouble.

I did. I was always giving her trouble. Once she had to send for my father to make me behave. Then she had to send for my mother to make my father behave.

He sounds like quite a lad, your father.

Oh, he is. He knows exactly how to make a peach cordial.

How?

He buys her a drink. But he wasn't always like that. Before he got married, they used to call him 'Jigsaw'.

Why 'Jigsaw'?

'Cos every time he was faced with a young lady he used to go to pieces. If my Dad hadn't been so shy and reserved, I'd be at least four years older.

So how did he actually get to meet your mother?

They were first cousins.

First cousins?

Yes, that's why I look so much alike.

I understand they're in the iron and steel business.

That's right – she irons and he steals. But at the time they got married, he was a jerry-builder and she was a chambermaid. It was a sort of marriage of convenience.

How did your father like children?

Boiled. One day a bloke came to the door and he said, 'I'm collecting for Doctor Barnardo's.'

So did your father give him anything?

Yes, five of us.

Maybe you weren't doing enough to please him.

I did try. I remember one cold wet night when he was coming in late from work, I lit a big roaring fire in his bedroom.

Was he pleased?

Of course he wasn't.

Why not?

There wasn't a fireplace in his bedroom. Finally, I could stand it no longer, so I ran away from home.

You ran away?

Yes, and it took them six months to find me.

Six months? Why?

They didn't look.

But wasn't your father upset at the thought of you leaving home?

Poor Dad, I remember his last words.

What were they?

'Rover,' he said.

'Rover?'

Yes, he'd always wanted a dog. 'Rover,' he said, 'when are you leaving?' And I said, 'I'm leaving tomorrow, Dad.'

And what did he say?

He said, 'Son, don't leave us tomorrow. Please.'

How sad.

'Leave us today.'

I wonder what made him like that.

I think it all stemmed from his disappointment when I was born.

Why? Did he want a girl?

No, he wanted a divorce. And from then on he always seemed to be disappointed in me. I remember once he said to me, 'How old are you, son?' And I said, 'I'm five.'

25

And what was his reply?

He was furious. He said, 'You ought to be ashamed of yourself. Why, when I was your age I was ten.' I realised I'd have to do better in the future.

So what did you do?

I said to him, 'Dad, can I have an encyclopaedia?'

Did he get you one?

No. He said, 'Of course you can't – you can walk to school like all the other kids.'

You must really have hated him.

I did. And what made me hate him more than anything else was the way he made me get up every morning at six o'clock to feed the chickens.

Why did you hate him so much for that?

Why did I hate him so much for it? We didn't have *any chickens.*

7 · Tee for two!

Y'know, I think my golf's improving.

You're right. You're missing the ball much closer than you used to.

What do you make my score so far?

Twenty-seven.

Twenty-seven? Not bad, eh?

No, but let's see how we get on with the second hole.

But seriously, what do you think of my game?

It's terrific. Mind you, I still prefer golf. You know what your main trouble is?

What?

You stand too close to the ball after you've hit it.

I still think I'm improving.

Oh, you are, you are. Why, only yesterday you hit the ball in one.

Absolutely! And anyway this is a terrible golf course. Just look at the state of it.

This isn't the course, you know – we left that half an hour ago.

Really? Is that why you keep looking at your watch?

This isn't a watch – this is a compass.

All right, so I'm not such a good golfer as you. What do you normally go round in?

Well, I usually wear this green sweater.

I like it. But what do you think would go best with these red and purple golf socks?

Hip boots?

I only bought them yesterday. I think they're terrific.

Yes, I just saw you putting them on in the dressing room. I can see why they're called golf socks.

Why?

Well, you've already got a hole-in-one. Mind you, it's not surprising, the way you stand to hit the ball.

The way *I* stand to hit the ball. What about *you*? You've no idea how to address the ball!

Well, at least I'm as polite to it as possible. I wish I could be as polite to my wife. She says if I don't give up golf, she'll leave me.

That's terrible.

I know – I'm really going to miss her.

It's the same with my doctor – he's just told me I can't play golf.

So he's played with you too, has he?

Incidentally, why aren't *you* playing golf with the doctor any more?

What! Would you play with a man who swears and curses with every shot he plays, who cheats in the bunkers and who's always putting down false scores on his cards? Would you?

Certainly not!

Well, neither will the doctor.

That's a pity 'cos the doctor plays a fair game of golf.

He does – if you watch him.

By the way, where did you find your caddy?

He was just standing by the clubhouse. I said to him, 'Are you any good at finding balls?' He said, 'Yes, I'm very good at finding balls.' I said, 'Good. Well, go and find me one and then we can get started.'

Well, he's certainly better than mine – I think I must have the world's worst caddy.

I doubt it. That would be too much of a coincidence. Anyway, let's get on with the next hole. I'll go first.

Okay. Tee the ball.

Of course I can see the ball – why all the baby talk?

Hey, nice shot! Now me. Great! Hey, did you see where it went?

I'm afraid I didn't.

Why not? I thought you were going to watch where it went.

You're right, I was.

So why didn't you?

Well, it doesn't normally go anywhere so I was taken a bit by surprise.

8 · Life with the lions!

Phew, this heat – it's terrible!

What's terrible?

The heat. It's so exhausting.

Hot? You call this hot?

Are you telling me you're not warm from the sun?

No – I'm Thomkins from the Telegraph.

You're a newspaper reporter?

That's right – and I remember one hot summer's day like this when I came into the office with no fewer than three scoops.

Really? What were they?

Chocolate, strawberry and vanilla. But this weather has nothing on Africa. I remember one day in Mombasa – it was 105° in the shade. But it didn't worry me.

Why not?

I stayed in the sun.

But didn't you faint eventually?

I did, but my wife, bless her, brought me to. Then I fainted again and the wife brought me two more.

It must have been scorching.

It was. We had to feed the chickens cracked ice to keep them from laying hard boiled eggs.

What were you doing out there?

I was doing a story on the water shortage.

But there's always a water shortage there.

I know, but this time it was serious. When I posted the story back I had to stick the stamp on with a pin.

What was your wife doing with you?

She was writing an African recipe book. We went out into the jungle looking for a cannibal tribe that eats a dish made from pygmies and snakes.

Ugh! What do they call it?

Snake and pygmy pie.

Did you have to go deep into the jungle?

Certainly, we went to places where the hand of man has never set foot. Deep, deep in the jungle, where the young girls all wear grass skirts and the young men spend all their time saving up for lawn-mowers.

Did you meet any wild animals?

Yes – one day we came face to face with a ferocious lion.

Did it give you a start?

I didn't need one. But I'd read a book about lions so I knew exactly which steps to take.

What?

Long ones. I ran to the nearest tree and climbed up it.

What about your wife?

She wasn't so lucky. The lion seized her in his jaws and carried her off.

Good heavens! What did she do?

She cried out, 'Shoot! Shoot!'

And did you?

I couldn't.

Why?

I'd run out of film.

Did you get down from the tree?

No, you get down from a swan – you get wood from a tree.

But had the lion devoured your wife?

No, fortunately he was a very sensible lion. Very careful about his diet.

How do you mean?

Well, he didn't want to eat anyone who might disagree with him – and my wife disagrees with everyone. The cannibal chief said to me, 'I don't like your wife.' I said, 'Leave her then – just eat the potatoes.'

But didn't he want to eat you?

No – he was very kind to me actually. He said, 'I'd like to have you for dinner.' He was very ambitious actually.

How do you mean?

He was always trying to get ahead.

But weren't you frightened?

32

No – they were afraid of me. They called me Iron Man. Until the rains came.

Then what did they call you?

Rusty Guts. Then I heard something which really cheered me up for a moment.

What was that?

That the chief had a very strict diet, he only liked beans.

Oh Good!

Human *beans!*

Oh dear!

We realised we had to escape. We ran into the jungle and lay down and I beat out a message on my wife's tum-tum.

You mean her tom-tom.

Listen – you beat what you want and I'll beat what I want.

And did help come?

Yes. Some Roman Catholic missionaries arrived and converted them. So, of course, they had to change their diet.

Naturally.

Now, on Fridays, they only eat fishermen.

9 · Fighting mad!

What are those medals you're wearing?

These are my military medals – I won them during the war.

I didn't know you'd won a couple of medals – what were they for?

Well, this one I got for saving two women.

Saving two women?

Yes, one for myself and one for the general.

And what about the other one?

Ah, yes, this was for saving the lives of the entire regiment.

What did you do?

I shot the cook.

I didn't realise you had such a distinguished war record.

Oh, yes. And I've got another one as a matter of fact.

Another distinguished war record?

Yes – Vera Lynn singing 'The White Cliffs of Dover'.

Is there a military tradition in your family?

Oh yes, I come from a very old military family. One of my ancestors fell at Waterloo.

Really?

Yes, someone pushed him off platform nine.

Where did you spend your war years?

Everywhere. I fought with Mountbatten in Burma, with Alexander in Tunis, with Monty at Alamein ... I couldn't get on with anyone. Hey, guess who was in the army with me?

Who?

Soldiers. No, we had a girl in our regiment, actually.

A girl?

Yes, she dressed up as a boy and joined our regiment.

But how did she get away with it? I mean, didn't they find out when she took a shower with the men?

Yes, but who was telling? But finally she was discovered and court-martialled.

36

And the presiding officer said to her, 'Private, you are sentenced to seven days on bread and water. How do you like that?'

And what did she say?

She said, 'Toasted, sir, if you don't mind.'

Did they let her stay in the regiment?

They did. For three more years she wore His Majesty's Uniform. Mind you, it fitted him better. And one day, with only one bullet left, she shot fifty-three German soldiers.

Fifty-three of them with one bullet?

Yes, they were coming at her in single file. Pity she wasn't with me when I was wounded.

Where were you wounded?

In the Dardanelles – very painful. No, I'll never forget my time in the Dardanelles. Especially the day I captured, single-handed, nearly three hundred Turks.

Wait a minute – the Dardanelles was the *First* World War. We weren't fighting the Turks in the Second World War.

I wondered why they came so quietly.

I don't believe you were wounded at all. Have you any scars?

No, but I can lend you a cigarette.

But did you actually see any action?

You're talking to a man who spent 1944 as driver and stage manager for Big Betty Braithwaite's All Girl Yodelling Belly Dancers and you're asking me if I saw any action. Please!

But did you meet anyone who actually put you in fear of your life?

Anyone apart from Big Betty Braithwaite, you mean?

Yes.

Well, there was the time I was fighting for this ridge against the German infantry. I dug myself a foxhole.

Was it very deep?

Was it deep? This foxhole was so deep it was just short of desertion. But my platoon was behind me as one man. And that's all there was -- one man. I said to him, 'Corporal, we have to take this ridge by nightfall.'

Why was that?

I was afraid of the dark. Then suddenly this gang of German soldiers appeared behind us.

What did you do?

What did I do? I proved to those Germans that this was no place for cowards.

How?

I ran like mad. But they soon caught up with us. And the fight started.

Were you struck in the mêlée?

No, I was struck in the ear-hole. Things looked pretty desperate. But then suddenly a parrot arrived with a note tied to its leg.

What did it say?

It said, 'There's a note tied to my leg.'

No, what did the *note* say?

It said, 'Percy the Parrot – messages delivered at reasonable prices.' Meanwhile this enormous German sergeant had thrown himself at me.

What did you do?

I rushed in with a left to the jaw and a right to the head, then an uppercut to the jaw and before he knew what had hit him . . .

Yes?

I was flat on my back. But I'll say this for him – he was a clean fighter.

How d'you mean?

He kept wiping the floor with me.

What a terrifying situation! How did you get out of it?

I did what any true fighting man would do in those circumstances.

What was that?

I surrendered.

But you must have escaped eventually.

I did. I asked them one night if I could go to the toilet and I slipped away from my guards. For seventeen days and nights I walked, hardly stopping to sleep, until finally, as I came over the brow of a hill, I saw the most beautiful sight of my life.

The British Army?

No, the toilet.

Well, you did your country proud. You were obviously a very brave soldier.

Thank you. My only regret was that I had but one life to give for my country.

A *very* brave soldier.

'Cos if I'd had two I'd have felt a helluva lot safer.

10 · Tight Christmas!

Well, the festive season is here again. Are you doing anything special?

Not really. We're having my mother-in-law for lunch on Christmas Day.

How nice.

Yes, I prefer chicken myself but times are hard. And I'm getting the wife a surprise present.

What is it?

A packet of cigarettes.

That's not much of a surprise.

It is – she's expecting a fur coat.

And what am *I* getting from you this Christmas?

Close your eyes and what do you see?

Nothing.

Well, that's what you're getting.

I just thought it would be nice if we exchanged presents.

Why not? I always exchange yours.

You don't strike me as being very sentimental about Christmas.

I'm extremely sentimental about Christmas, actually. Every Christmas Eve I still take my socks off and stand them in front of the fireplace.

But Christmas doesn't seem the same as it was when we were kids.

Yes, it was different then somehow. I can see it all now – my father sitting in front of the fire roasting his chestnuts. My brother playing with his new yo.

His new yo?

Yes, my parents couldn't afford a yo-yo.

You must have been very poor.

We were. The wolf was at the door so often we used to call him Rover. And we could hardly ever afford a turkey. One year, I remember, things were so bad my father gave the budgie a chest expander.

So you always tried to have some sort of bird?

Not always. I remember one Christmas dinner a terrible row breaking out over who would have the middle cut of the sardine.

Was it a big family?

41

I'll say. I was the fourteenth out of thirteen children. And born in a pretty tough area too. If you saw a cat with a tail on round our way, you knew he was a tourist. Even the doctor who delivered me was poor – his stethoscope was on a party line.

Weren't you a twin?

I was – our parents couldn't afford to have us one at a time.

I suppose you could share the same nappy.

That's right, it was the only way to make ends meet.

Things must have been pretty rough.

You bet – we couldn't afford talcum powder.

And I suppose you wore your brother's hand-me-downs?

I did. And that was really tough.

Why?

He was still wearing them.

That must have been difficult.

Not really – we weren't exactly tubby. I had two older brothers who were so thin they went around in the same pair of trousers.

That *is* thin.

That's nothing. When I was nine years old, my legs were so thin, my mother used them as knitting needles. And my head was so thin, my eyes were in single file.

But it was a loving home, that's the main thing.

Absolutely. Especially at Christmas. I remember one year my parents couldn't afford to buy me the pair of shoes they'd promised me.

So what did they do?

They painted my feet black and laced up my toes.

Aah! Christmas always brings the best out in people, doesn't it?

Well, you tell my wife that.

Why, is she giving you trouble?

I'll say. She said to me today, 'You've done absolutely nothing to help with the Christmas dinner. Absolutely nothing.'

What did you say to that?

I said, 'What! Look at the turkey – I bought it, I've plucked it and I've stuffed it!'

Good for you!

Now, all she's got to do is kill it and put it in the oven.

11 · School daze!

Ladies and Gentlemen, a recitation: 'There is nothing that I find more beguiling ...'

Excuse me, what time is it?

Do you mind! You've got a watch anyway.

I know I have, but I've just dropped it.

You mean it stopped when it hit the floor?

Well, you didn't expect it to go straight through, did you?

Of course I didn't, stupid.

Don't you call me stupid! I've got more brains in my little finger than I've got in my whole head.

'There is nothing that I find more beguiling
Than the face of a child when it is smiling ...'

You're right! Kids – I love 'em.

What do you know about children anyway?

Quite a lot, actually. I used to be one myself.

The way you're acting, I think you probably still are.

If you say that again I'll be forced to put down my lolly and belt you one.

You and who else?

Me and my brother. Okay?

I didn't know you had a brother.

Of course you did. I've told you before, my parents had three children. One of each.

What are their names?

Well, there's my brother – he's named after my father.

What do you call him?

Dad. And there's my sister, Onyx.

Onyx? Why did they call her Onyx?

'Cos she was Onyxpected. She was one of the prettiest babies in our town.

Really? Where did she first see the light of day?

Well, she first saw the light of day in Stockport. She was actually born two years earlier in Manchester.

46

Manchester? I think Manchester's a great place.

So do I. But all I remember about Manchester in those days was being woken up in the morning by the sounds of birds coughing. It was no place for sissies – all the canaries round our way sang baritone.

I had a pretty tough childhood myself, you know. At the age of five I was left an orphan.

That's ridiculous! What could a five year old do with an orphan? Anyway, our family was so tough, I was shaving when I was three years old.

That's crazy, how can a three year old shave?

By standing in the sink.

You were lucky to have a sink to stand in. All we had was an outside loo. It was no wonder that by the time I was nine I had chronic influenza.

Only chronic influenza! Look, when I was eleven I had a really terrible time. First I got tonsillitis which was followed by pneumonia. Then I got appendicitis, and that was followed by poliomyelitis. After that I got neuritis and finally ended up with bronchitis. Then they gave me antitoxins and hydrotherapy.

That's terrible!

I know. To give an eleven year old a spelling test like that!

They must have thought you were very clever at school.

They did. Every time the teacher asked a question, I was the first to put up my hand.

That *was* clever.

You bet – and by the time I got back, the question had been answered.

What was your favourite subject at school?

Oh, without a doubt, Arith ... Arithnat ... Arithmap ... History.

Really? Mine was singing.

Singing? You couldn't carry a tune in an armoured car!

I'll have you know I come from a very musical family. We were all singers at home.

So were we – there was no lock on the toilet door. Yes, they were tough times all right. It's no wonder people were surprised that I always had a smile on my face as a kid.

For all those years, through thick and thin, you kept smiling?

I couldn't help it.

Why was that?

I'd swallowed a banana sideways.

12 · Girl talk!

Who was that lady I seen you with last night?

You mean 'I saw'.

Sorry. Who was that eyesore I seen you with last night?

Do you mind! When I first saw her at the Palais, she was easily the prettiest thing on the floor.

Yes, I can see her now, lying there.

She's fantastic! She reads a lot, likes classical music and modern art and loves visiting museums.

Don't worry, nobody's perfect.

Phew! Is she a girl! Is ... she ... a ... girl!!

That's what I was wondering.

When I went to pick her up last night, she opened the door in her négligé!

That's a funny place to have a door.

I could see immediately why she was once taken for Raquel Welch.

She may have been taken for Raquel Welch, but I bet they brought her back in a hurry.

Within ten minutes, she'd put her arms around me three times.

Well, I thought she had long arms but that's ridiculous!

She's amazing! She's got everything a man could want.

Big muscles, a beard, a handle-bar moustache ...

Her eyes are like two limpid pools!

... and her nose is like a diving board!

Her ears are like petals.

Bicycle petals!

Her cheeks are like peaches.

Football peaches!

And her teeth are like stars.

They come out at night!

But her eyes especially! They're so romantic!

I know – I could tell from the way they snuggled up to each other.

And her legs!

49

Her legs! At least no-one can say she's bow-legged.

Why?

She's knock-kneed.

What do you mean?

Look, that girl has got two of the ugliest legs in town!

How do you know?

I've counted them.

You've never seen them!

I have. I saw her in town last week wearing a mini-skirt. Honestly, the last time I saw legs like that, there was a message tied to them! And those open-toed shoes she wears!

They're lovely!

And very useful, too.

How d'you mean?

I noticed her last night – with those open-toed shoes, she can pick up cigarette ends without bending down.

Don't be stupid! She doesn't need to do that!

Not while you're doing it for her, I suppose.

But she wouldn't do it anyway, she's a lady!

Well, I don't know about that. But she is a bit hoity-toity.

Hoity-toity?

Yes. Or let's put it this way – she's extremely hoity but she'll never see toity again.

I'm not talking to you any more. You're just jealous.

Jealous?

Yes, jealous of my good looks ...

Your good looks! I'm telling you, with a face like that you ought to be in radio!

... and jealous of my success with women.

Your success with women?

Certainly – when I kiss a girl, she certainly knows she's been kissed.

She knows she's been kissed?

Yes.

Why, who tells her?

13 · Beside the seaside, beside the sea!

Ladies and gentlemen, it's marvellous to be here, absolutely marvellous!

It's fantastic to be here. Fantastic! Where are we?

We're at Littleton-on-Sea. And we're having a wonderful time, aren't we?

Are we?

Of course we are. What's that you've got there?

A lobster.

A lobster? Are you taking it home for tea?

No, it's had its tea – now I'm taking it to the pictures.

It's a lovely place, Littleton, isn't it? How do you find the weather?

I just go outside and there it is.

No, what I mean is, the weather's been quite nice, hasn't it?

It's been lovely, if you happen to be a sponge. It was raining so hard yesterday, people were jumping into the sea to save themselves from drowning. I almost got back on the train and went straight home.

Incidentally, how was your trip down?

It was fine. It started off badly, mind.

How d'you mean?

Well, I went to Waterloo and asked for a return ticket. And the bloke said, 'Where to?' And I said, 'Back here, of course.'

Then what?

Then he said, 'That'll be £3.50. Change at Melchester.' And I said, 'I'll have my change here *if you don't mind!'*

Good for you! How was the journey itself?

Terrible! I felt sick, sitting all that way with my back to the engine.

Why didn't you ask the person sitting opposite to change places?

I couldn't – there was no-one there!

I bet you were glad to get here.

You're telling me! I stood outside the station and took a deep breath of that fresh seaside air.

Marvellous!

One lung said to the other, 'That's the stuff I've been telling you about!'

Great!

Then I went directly to the beach, stripped off and ran straight into the sea.

Did it come up to your expectations?

Just past them actually – that's the trouble with being so short. Then, would you believe it, a crab bit my toe!

Which one?

I don't know – all crabs look alike to me. I could hardly walk so I decided to take a donkey ride. The bloke said, 'Don't take the one on the end – the rest'll fall over.' I said to him, 'Can I hire this donkey?' He said, 'Yes, there's a screw under the saddle.'

So the donkey took you home?

No, just as far as the bus stop. I got on the bus and I said to the driver, 'Do you stop at the Ritz Hotel?' And he said, 'What, on my wages?'

Did you ask him again?

Yes, I said, 'Look, does this bus stop at the harbour?' He said, 'If it doesn't, there's going to be one hell of a splash!'

Didn't you explain to him that the Ritz Hotel is right next door to the harbour?

I did. And I invited him to drop in any time he liked. Preferably when the tide was out.

And when the life-guard's looking in the opposite direction!

Did you know I used to be a life-guard?

Really? When?

Last summer.

What did you do?

I saved women.

What for?

The winter.

Didn't you help any men?

Yes, I gave them the occasional woman. One day I had to rescue a drunken mermaid.

57

A drunken mermaid?

Yes, she'd had so much whiskey on the rocks, she'd fallen into the sea.

How drunk was she?

She was absolutely legless. I pulled her onto the beach and gave her artificial recreation.

You mean artificial *respiration*. Recreation is when you have fun.

I'm no fool. She had a fabulous figure, too.

Really?

Yes, thirty-six, twenty-three, eighty-five pence a pound. Hey, have you heard the one about the mermaid who climbs onto this rock, takes her teeth out, whips out a harmonica and starts playing 'God Save The Queen'? Have you heard it?

No.

Well, you should have done.

Why?

It's the National Anthem.

14 · Camping about!

Excuse me, are you the manager of this holiday camp?

I certainly am, sir – Bobkins' Holiday Camps at your service! You're one of our earliest holiday-makers this year. The camp has only been open a week.

I know – I like to get in early while the sheets are still clean.

Anyway, sir, can I help you?

Yes, it's about the roof of my chalet.

What about it?

I'd like one.

Certainly, sir. But apart from that, everything is satisfactory?

Well, the walls are a bit thin.

You mean you can hear the radio next door?

It's worse than that – I can see their television! And when I opened the oven door the other day to look at the Sunday joint, I caught the bloke next door dipping his bread in my gravy. And what a place to have a holiday camp!

Melmouth-on-Sea, sir? It's the loveliest resort!

More like the last *resort! Last Monday the tide went out and it hasn't bothered to come back yet.*

And have you any *more* complaints, sir?

No, it doesn't matter. I was going to complain about the lack of furniture in my chalet but you'll just accuse me of getting up on the wrong side of the floor this morning.

Do you have anything *good* to say about Bobkins' Holiday Camp, sir?

Well, the girls are pretty good here.

Oh yes, we always say you can't beat the girls at Bobkins'!

I know – I've read the rules.

So how many girls have you been out with so far?

Would you believe twenty-three?

No, I wouldn't.

Five?

No.

All right – one. But what a girl!

Did you meet her at the late night pyjama party?

Yes, everyone was standing round talking about the weather.

The weather?

Yes – whether they should or whether they shouldn't.

So who introduced you?

Her brother. He said, 'Do you know my sister May?' I said, 'No, I didn't, but thanks for the tip.'

May? Didn't she go in for our Beauty Competition?

That's right – she was voted Miss Demeanour 1979.

I remember her bikini.

That's right. She was wearing her nuclear bathing costume.

Nuclear bathing costume?

Yes – sixty per cent fall-out! She certainly showed those judges a thing or two.

So what happened after the pyjama party?

I took her back to her chalet. As we left the dance hall, I put her head on my shoulders.

Yes!

Someone else was carrying her feet.

Yes!

When we got to her chalet, I said, 'May, may,' I said, 'May I hold your hand?'

And she said?

'I'll manage thank you very much, it's not very heavy.'

Did you go in?

We did. And I said to her, 'Why don't you slip into something cooler?'

And did she?

Yes – she got into the fridge. And then the AA man came round.

The AA man? In Bobkins' Holiday Camp? What was he doing?

He was going, ''ay, 'ay, you can't do that! 'ay, 'ay, cut that out!' And so on.

Did he bang on your door?

Yes. He said, 'Have you got a lady in there?'

So what did you say?

I said, 'Hang on, I'll ask her.' But we had a wonderful evening.

62

Did you?

Mind your own business. She's a lovely girl, though. I'd like to marry her, but her family objects.

Her family?

Yes, her husband and four kids.

That's too bad.

I know. I'm glad I'm going home tomorrow, it'll help me forget about her.

But you can't leave tomorrow. You booked into Bobkins' Holiday Camp for a fortnight and you've only been here seven days.

But it's all right, I can go. They said I could.

How come?

They've given me a week off for good behaviour.

15 · Marry making!

Ladies and gentlemen, 'The Wedding', a recitation:

It seems like only yesterday that I got married. I wish it was tomorrow – I'd call the whole thing off.

To continue: 'On her finger a ring, on her face a smile,
The radiant bride walks down the aisle ...'

It was a love match pure and simple. I was pure and she was simple.

Do you mind! I'm trying to recite a poem ...

The trouble was, I went into marriage with both eyes closed – her father closed one and her brother closed the other.

Excuse me ...

I think they must have still been annoyed about our first wedding.

Your *first* wedding?

Yes, it was a very quiet affair – I didn't turn up. I ought to have known from the first time I met her. I said, 'When are you thinking of getting married?' She said, 'All the time.'

Where did you meet her anyway?

I met her at a party. We were playing Chef's Knock.

Chef's Knock?

Yes, it's like Postman's Knock but you make more of a meal of it. I smiled at her. She smiled back.

What followed?

I did. She, being a lady, dropped her eyelids. I, being a gentleman, picked them up.

How gallant!

Absolutely. Then, later that night, as I was walking her home, I saved her from being attacked.

How?

I controlled myself.

Did you meet her parents?

Only her father.

Did he say anything?

Yes. He said, 'Young man, are your intentions honourable or dishonourable?'

64

And you said?

'You mean to say I've got a choice?'

So where was her mother?

She was out at the pictures, watching a cowboy film.

A cowboy film?

Yes, she's mad about cowboys. She's the only woman I know with spurs on her slippers. She spends two nights a week standing in front of the mirror, trying to beat herself to the draw.

How fascinating. But it's got nothing to do with what I came here tonight to do, which was to recite my poem, 'The Wedding'.

Of course it was. Go ahead.

' 'Twas a wondrous sight that I will ne'er forget ...'

'As she paused by a candle – and lit a cigarette.'

Thank you very much! You've ruined a poetical gem. I hope you're pleased with yourself!

Well, a bit. But not as pleased as I was the day we decided to get married. Would you like to hear how I asked her father for his daughter's hand in marriage?

You're going to tell me anyway.

Am I? Oh, all right. If you insist. I said, 'Sir, the bright sunshine of your daughter's smile has dispelled the dark clouds of my depression!' He said, 'Are you proposing or is this the weather forecast?' Good, eh?

Terrific.

I said, 'I would like your daughter for my wife.' He said, 'But I've never even seen your wife. Bring her round and we'll talk about it.'

You got through to him eventually?

Yes – he said, 'So you want to marry my daughter? Don't you think you'd better see my wife first?' I said, 'I have, sir and I still want to marry your daughter.'

You *did* tell the mother, tho'.

I did, and she was really excited. She said, 'Is it going to be a white wedding?' I said, 'Yes, if it snows.'

And did it?

No, it was a lovely day. All our friends were there, throwing old shoes.

How romantic!

66

And her father was there – trying them on. The bride almost tripped over him walking down the aisle.

Didn't she see him?

No. You see, she used to be an usherette.

So?

So she was walking down the aisle backwards.

Where did you have the reception?

At my Auntie Vera's place. What a party! Especially when Auntie Vera disappeared with the vicar.

Where did they go?

I've no idea – but they say they found his vest in her pantry ...

No!

... and her pants in his vestry.

That's terrible!

I know. But, over all, it was a truly memorable day, because I never knew what real happiness was until I got married.

Really?

Yes – and by then it was too late.

16 · Honeymoonshine!

Well, hello! How are you?

Fine, thanks – how are *you?*

Terrific!

Well, I must be off. See you!

Wait a minute, wait a minute! Where are you off to?

I'm going to the travel agent to book my summer holiday.

Really? Where are you going?

Don't know yet – somewhere foreign.

So what's wrong with England?

Nothing, I just like being abroad.

Really? I prefer being a chap, myself. But I really don't see the appeal of foreign countries. What all those foreigners see in them, I just don't know.

What do you know about it anyway? Your idea of an exciting holiday is a cycling tour of Scarborough.

Oh, really? Well it might interest you to know that I returned yesterday from a holiday in Europe.

Really? Where did you go?

Where did I go? Ooh lah lah, mais oui, mais non, d'accord! Spain.

What did you go to Spain for?

Thirty-five pounds return. It was a honeymoon special.

A honeymoon special? How long have you been married?

Three weeks. And they said it wouldn't last.

But five weeks ago you didn't even have a girlfriend.

I know – our courtship was fast and furious.

Really?

Yes – I was fast and she was furious.

And was it *your* idea to get married?

Yes. Fortunately, she's got a stutter.

Fortunately?

Yes, 'cos by the time she said she wouldn't, she had.

70

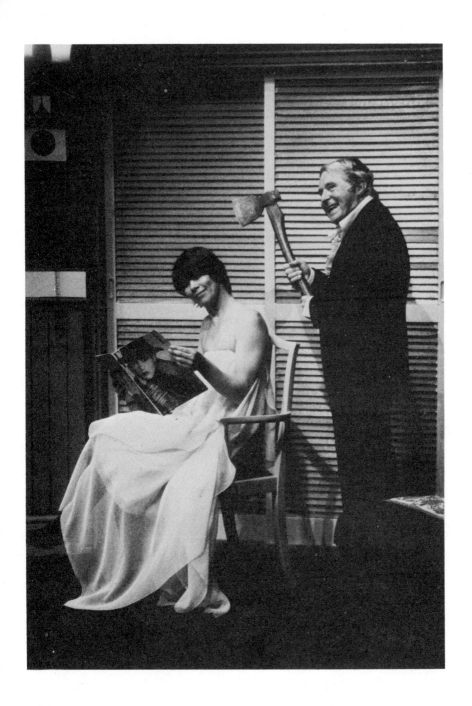

But I didn't even hear about the wedding.

Well, it was a very quiet affair – the vicar had laryngitis. But it was an unforgettable occasion. You have never seen two happier people.

Aah!

Her parents. We were already arguing about our honeymoon.

What was the problem?

Well, I wanted to take her on a trip round the world. But she wanted to go somewhere else.

So what made you go to Spain?

We heard about this cheap flight for honeymooners. Mind you, it was cheap – the plane was so old it had an outside toilet.

Were you nervous?

The wife was. She said to the pilot, 'You will bring us down safely, won't you?'

What did he say?

He said, 'Don't worry, madam – I've never left anyone up there yet.'

Was it a special honeymooners' hotel?

From the behaviour of our fellow guests, yes.

How do you mean?

Well, they all started yawning at six o'clock in the evening.

But I love those foreign hotels! Wasn't there something about the place that makes you simply itch to get back?

Yes – fleas. The manager said, 'You won't find a single flea in any of my beds.' He was right – they were all married with families!

What sort of room did you have?

It was quite nice actually. We had a double room with bath – pity about them being in separate buildings. I would have complained but I didn't know enough Spanish.

Didn't you know *any* Spanish?

I knew two words and they reckon that's all you need to know for honeymooning in Spain.

And what are they?

'Mañana' – that means 'Tomorrow'. And, 'Pyjama' – that means 'Tonight'.

So at least you've no complaints in that area?

No – it was all wonderfully romantic. Every night we'd sit on the settee, with the moonlight streaming in through the holes in the ceiling while she ran her fingers through my money.

And what about the food, that delicious Spanish food? I've had some Spanish food that's been almost heavenly!

Well, most of ours was almost edible. We went out for a special meal one night, tho'. It was a very posh restaurant. Just to impress the wife, I ordered the whole meal in French. Even the waiter was surprised.

Really?

Yes – it was a Chinese restaurant.

Was it good value?

Terrific value. For about a pound each, they serve you all the food you can eat.

Fantastic!

The trouble is, they only give you one chopstick.

Still, it sounds like a terrific place to go.

It's a marvellous place to go. But a lousy place to eat.

Didn't you try any *Spanish* restaurants?

Well, just outside town there was this little place with a sign that said, 'Topless Bar'. So we went in there.

You took your wife into a topless bar?

Yes. I mean – when you've seen two you've seen them all. Anyway, it turned out to be a bit of a disappointment.

How come?

Turned out to be a cafe with no roof on. Still, we decided to eat there. But just as they brought the food, it started to rain.

Oh no!

Oh yes – it took us an hour and a half to finish the soup! I'm sticking to Bridlington next year. I've had enough of foreign travel. Same as a bloke at work.

What happened to him?

He went in for a competition and won a trip to China.

Lucky chap.

Yes. He's out there now trying to win a trip back.

17 · The dumb waiter!

Ah, good evening, I've been looking forward to patronising this restaurant.

Good evening, sir – and now we are looking forward to patronising you.

Tell me – do you serve crabs?

We serve anyone, sir. Take a seat.

Thank you. Boy, I'm so hungry I could eat a horse.

You've certainly come to the right place, sir.

Hey, this water's a bit cloudy.

There's nothing wrong with the water, sir, it's just a dirty glass.

Is this bread fresh?

I'll say it's fresh – we've had to put it on the top shelf to keep it away from the tarts.

What's the soup like?

Delicious, sir. I'm going to have some myself if there's any left.

All right – I'll join you in a bowl of soup.

Well, I hope there's room for both of us. Soup coming up!

Now, what else? Have you any wild duck?

No, sir – but we've got a tame one we could aggravate for you.

Er, no thanks. Have you got pig's trotters?

No, sir – flat feet.

I'll have the mixed grill.

Certainly, sir.

And make the chops lean!

Of course, sir – which way? Here's your soup.

Thank you. Incidentally, waiter, I don't like all the flies in this dining-room.

Well, point out the ones you don't like, sir, and I'll chase them out for you.

Wait a minute! This plate's wet!

That's your soup, sir.

But wait a minute – there's a fly in my soup!

They don't care what they eat, do they, sir?

But what's it doing there?

It looks like the breaststroke to me, sir.

I can't believe it! A fly in my soup!

Don't make a fuss, sir, they'll all want one.

But it looks like it's dead!

Yes, it's the heat that kills them.

Just take it away – I don't want it.

Certainly, sir. Here's your mixed grill.

Thank you. Hey, what's your thumb doing on my steak?

I don't want it to fall on the floor again, sir.

You know something? This egg smells bad.

Well, don't blame me – I only laid the table.

And I can't cut this steak.

Sorry, sir, I'll get you a knife sharpener.

I don't want a knife sharpener, I want the manager! I can't eat this food.

There's no use – he wouldn't eat it either.

Look at this sausage! It's got meat in one end and bread in the other.

I'm sorry, sir, but these days it's hard to make both ends meat.

But this food isn't fit for a pig!

Well, wait a minute – I'll bring you some that is. Here's your coffee, anyway.

Thank you. Yecchhh! This coffee tastes like tea!

I'm sorry, sir, I must have given you the cocoa instead. Here – this is the coffee.

Thank you. Yecchhh! *This* coffee tastes like mud!

I'm not surprised – it was ground only half an hour ago.

Is this my bill?

Yes, sir.

I'm terribly sorry – it looks as if I've got just enough money to pay for the dinner but I've got nothing to tip you with.

Let me add that bill up again, sir.

18. Salad of the bad cafe!

Excuse me, are you the same waiter who showed me to my table and gave me the menu?

Yes, sir.

Well, you don't look a day older.

I assume you do have a reservation, sir.

Of course I don't. What do you think I am – a Red Indian? Can I please order?

Certainly, sir, everything's on the menu.

So I see – bring me a clean one. In the meantime I want two underdone sausages, three rashers of bacon burnt to a cinder, a portion of peas reduced to a thick green mush and a shrivelled-up baked potato.

But sir, I can't serve that!

Why not? You did yesterday! And do you know what I had for lunch the day before?

No, sir?

Three-quarters of an hour. Anyway, tell me what you've got.

Well, sir, today I have fried liver, boiled tongue, stewed kidneys and pig's feet.

Don't tell me your ailments – I came here to eat. Is the filet steak tender?

As tender as a woman's heart, sir.

Then bring me some bacon. And last week when I was here I had some rump steak.

Yes, sir, and will you have the same today?

Well, I might as well, if no one else is using it.

And a soup, sir?

Yes – that chap over there is having soup and it sounds delicious. What sort is it?

It's bean soup, sir.

I don't care what it's been – what is it now? Forget the soup, do you have frog's legs?

Yes, sir.

Good – hop over to the counter and get my bacon.

Certainly, sir.

And do you have any stewed prunes?

Yes, sir.

Well, give them some black coffee to sober them up. Yecchhh! This bacon tastes terrible. It must be bad.

That's impossible, sir. It was cured only last week.

Then it must have had a relapse.

But this is the best bacon we've had for years, sir.

Then you should have given me some you've had more recently. And another thing, waiter.

Don't tell me, sir – you've found something fresh to complain about.

If it was fresh, I wouldn't complain about it. It's this steak.

Ah yes, sir – how did you find it?

I just moved this potato and there it was. Altogether a very disappointing meal, I'm afraid.

Well, I'm very sorry to hear that, sir, because the chef really put his heart into it.

I thought there was a funny taste there somewhere. Have you any cheese to finish with?

Only this, sir.

No thanks.

But it's gruyere, sir.

I don't care where it grew – I just don't like it. Just bring me my bill.

Certainly, sir. I trust you enjoyed your meal.

Well, I would enjoy the food here but for one small fault.

What's that, sir?

It's inedible. But don't get me wrong – I've nothing but admiration for this restaurant.

Oh, thank you, sir.

And I've very little of that.

19 · Losing his patients!

Doctor, I don't know what's wrong with me. Do you think I'll ever get better?

I don't know – let me feel your purse.

But Doctor ...

Sit down and tell me all about it ...

Doctor, I'm not a private patient. I'm on the National Health.

... in less than two minutes.

Well, for a start I've got this terrible insomnia.

Well, I wouldn't lose any sleep over it. Why don't you try eating something before you go to bed.

But Doctor – two months ago you told me never to eat anything before going to bed.

But that was two months ago – medical science has made enormous strides since then.

Have you any other advice?

Yes. Sleep nearer the edge of the bed. You'll soon drop off.

And if that doesn't work?

Try talking to yourself.

And now my memory seems to be going. What shall I do?

Try and forget about it.

And another thing – it seems that people just don't notice me any more.

Next patient, please!

Then there's this terrible cold I've got.

Yes, it's a nasty cough – have you had it before?

Yes.

Well, now you've got it again.

I've been in bed all day with a hot water bottle and a thermometer in my mouth.

Well, there's certainly room enough for both.

But what should I take for my cold?

Don't refuse any offer.

But how can I stop it spreading from my head to my chest?

Tie a knot in your throat. And, incidentally, you need new glasses.

How do you know?

I could tell as soon as you walked through that window.

New glasses? Does that mean I'm going to have to be examined all over again?

No, just your eyes.

Oh, good. And do you know, last week I was hit by a bus?

Well, it's no wonder you're feeling a bit run down.

Well, I broke a couple of ribs and now I keep getting this stitch in my side.

Stitch? That's fine – it just shows that the bones are knitting.

But I'm beginning to think I broke my neck at the same time.

Broken your neck? Well, keep your chin up.

Honestly, I feel like every bone in my body is aching.

Then be glad you're not a herring.

And I've got a terrible pain in my left foot.

Well, try walking with the other one.

Well, aren't you going to examine me?

Certainly. Go over to the window and put your tongue out.

Why?

'Cos I don't like the bloke who lives opposite. Tell me – when you get up in the morning, do you feel all depressed and have a furry tongue and a pain in the middle of your shoulders?

Yes, that's right, I do.

Well, so do I. I wonder what it is. Incidentally, your hair is falling out – do you want me to give you something to keep it in?

Oh, yes please, Doctor.

Well, try this shoebox.

Thank you. Well, Doctor – how do you think I stand?

I don't know – it's a miracle.

But do you think I'll live?

Well, yes – but ...

But what?

... but I don't advise it.

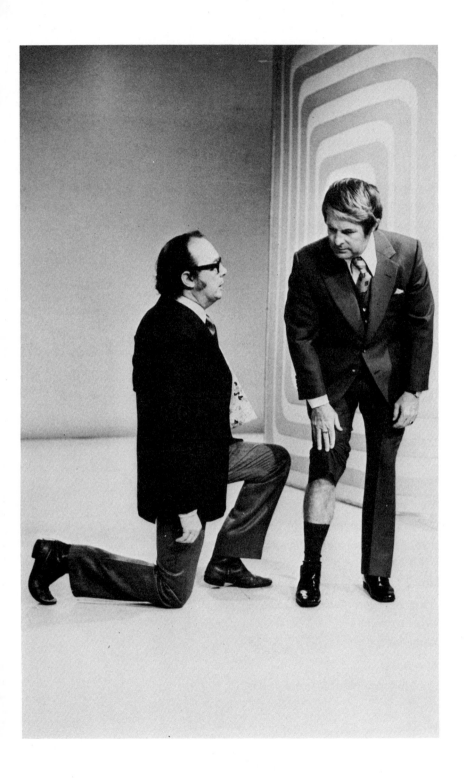

20 · Oh doctor!

Ah, come in! You're coughing more easily this morning.

I should be – I've been practising all night.

But aren't you taking the medicine I gave you.

No. I tasted it and I decided to keep coughing.

But haven't you followed my advice for getting rid of a cold – to drink frozen orange juice after a hot bath?

Yes, but I haven't finished drinking the hot bath yet. Look out, I'm going to sneeze!

At who?

Atchoo!!

Well, I've got a cold too, so cheer up, I've got the same complaint as you.

True, but you are lucky in one respect.

What's that?

You don't have the same doctor.

Let's examine you. Stick your tongue out and say, 'Ah.'

Ah.

Well, your tongue looks all right but why the postage stamp?

So that's where I left it.

Has anyone taken your pulse?

No, I've still got it.

Do you take any exercise?

Well, I was out last week four nights running. And the fifth night I gave myself a bad back.

How?

It was my wife's fault – she made me carry the mangle from the cellar to the attic.

What for?

To paint it.

Couldn't you paint it in the cellar?

No.

Why?

The paint was in the attic.

Do you suffer from rheumatism?

Yes – what else can you do with it?

Have you ever been troubled with diphtheria?

Only when I've tried to spell it.

Well, I can't tell what's wrong with you. I think it's drink.

Okay – I'll come back when you're sober.

Maybe you'd better give me a specimen.

Okay.

If you could just fill that bottle over there.

From here?

No – take it home with you and bring it back tomorrow.

I hope I remember. My memory's terrible these days.

Tell me all about it.

All about what?

About your memory.

Oh, yes. There are three things I can't remember. I can't remember names, I can't remember faces ...

Yes?

... and I can't remember what the third thing is.

Can you remember if your eyes have been checked before?

No, they've always been blue.

Why do you wear those glasses?

I've got spots before my eyes.

And do the glasses help?

Yes – the spots are much bigger now.

Maybe you've got weak eyesight.

That's ridiculous – on a clear day I can see my glasses. Oh dear, I'm beginning to feel like a steering-wheel again.

A steering-wheel? How do you mean?

Well, I keep getting these awful turns. Sometimes I feel like I've got one foot in the grate.

You mean the grave.

No, I'm going to be cremated. But then I remember I come from a family of long livers.

Really?

Yes – my father had a liver two feet long.

Maybe you're suffering from insomnia. How did you sleep last night?

Oh, lying down as usual. Mind you, I used to snore so loud I woke myself up. But I've cured that.

How?

I'm sleeping in the room next door. Oh, incidentally, could you give me some sleeping pills for the wife.

Why?

She keeps waking up. But the main thing is, Doctor, I want you to reassure me. When all this clears up, will I be able to play tennis?

Of course you will!

That's marvellous – I never could before.

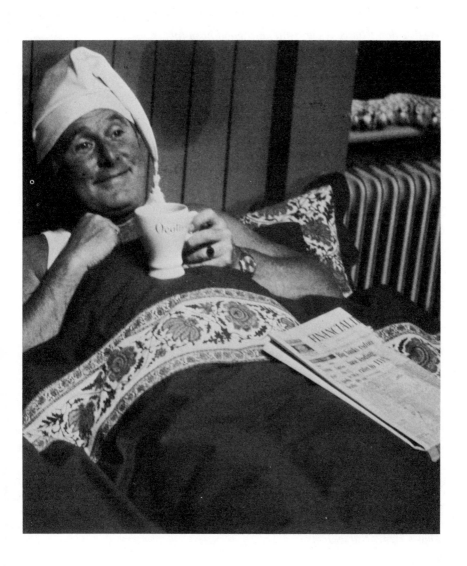

21 · Wards and all!

You know, if I have to be in hospital, this is as good a place to be as any.

Well, I don't think it can be a very good hospital.

Why's that?

Well, all the patients are ill. Look at that bloke over there, for instance – he's got terrible trouble with his head.

What sort of trouble with his head?

I don't know exactly but he's had it on and off since he was a kid. And the bloke in the end bed's got a glass eye.

Did he tell you?

No, it just came out in the conversation. And the bloke who was in that bed before you – he was in here for five weeks having all sorts of treatment.

But they finally straightened him out?

Yes – they buried him yesterday.

What about him over there?

He's having terrible pain from his wooden leg.

But how can a wooden leg give you pain?

His wife keeps hitting him over the head with it.

But why doesn't he just take it away from her?

He does – then she just hits him with his other one.

He's got *two* wooden legs?

Yes – he hasn't got a leg to stand on. Word has it that he's going to be in here for quite a long time.

Why, have you seen his doctor?

No, I've seen his nurse.

Not the blonde one?

That's right, Nurse Tonsils.

Tonsils?

Yes, all the doctors want to take her out. But she's engaged to an X-ray specialist.

An X-ray specialist?

Yes. I can't think what he sees in her.

The nurse I like is that little redhead downstairs. It would be a delight to be nursed by a girl like her.

A delight? It would be a miracle – she's in the maternity ward.

I dreamed about her last night. I dreamed she made me eat this *enormous* marshmallow. It took me ages to get it down – it was terrible!

Well, you're all right now, but where's your pillow?

Oh no!

It's no wonder you're feeling a little down in the mouth. Excuse me a moment.

Hey – why are you jumping up and down like that?

The doctor just gave me some medicine and he forgot to shake the bottle.

Incidentally, why did you ask him to leave you until last when he's making his rounds?

I like to give him time for his hands to warm up. You know what – I should have come in here two weeks ago.

Why didn't you?

I was ill.

What was wrong?

Well, my housemaid's knee has been giving me trouble.

Your housemaid's knee?

Yes – the wife caught me sitting on it. I suppose I'll just have to try and forget about her.

The housemaid?

No, the wife. Still, I won't find it difficult – I can't remember anything these days. In fact I went to see the specialist last week about my loss of memory.

What did he do?

He made me pay him in advance. My wife's got a terrible memory, too.

Really?

Yes – she never forgets a thing. I ought to send her to the same specialist.

Have you ever been to him before?

Yes.

What for?

Thirty-five guineas.

No – I mean, what did you have?

87

Only twenty-*five guineas.*

You still don't understand – what was your complaint?

That the bill was too high. Reminds me of the time I went to see the specialist about my slipped disc.

What happened?

He said he'd have me back on my feet in a fortnight.

And did he?

Yes – I had to sell the car to pay him. What are you *in here for anyway?*

I fell out of a fifth storey window.

Well, you don't look too bad. I suppose the ground must have broken your fall.

Actually I broke my leg in three places.

Didn't anyone warn you about going to those places?

What happened to *you* anyway?

Well, I was walking past this building site when this enormous brick came hurtling down – missing my shoulder by that *much.*

So why are you in here?

'Cos it landed smack on the top of my head.

22 · Boxers rule, KO?

Did you see the big fight on television last night?

Yes.

Wasn't the champ fantastic?

Fantastic? He was terrible! That bloke couldn't hit a phone box from inside it. He's useless!

Useless? What do *you* know about it anyway?

What do I know about it? You're only talking to the ex-Lightweight Champion of Leicester, that's all.

Heavens! I didn't know you were a boxer.

I wasn't – I was a coal merchant. But actually, I was a pretty handy fighter in my youth. I could lick any man with one hand.

Really?

Yes. Unfortunately, I could never find anyone with one hand who wanted a fight. All the same, I was a pretty colourful fighter.

How do you mean?

I was black and blue all over. My best punch was my rabbit punch.

Yes?

But they wouldn't let me fight rabbits.

Do you remember your first fight?

I remember it like I remember my last *fight. No wonder – it was the same fight.*

Were you nervous in the dressing-room?

I was terrified. The referee came in and he said, 'You're shaking like a leaf.' I said, 'How do you want me to shake?' He said, 'Take your dressing-gown off.' I did. And then he looked at me for a full thirty seconds.

What did he say?

He said, 'You've still got time to go home and get your body.' Then he made me take out the horseshoe.

The horseshoe?

Yes – I'd just put it in my glove.

What for?

For good luck.

It must be a long walk from the dressing-room to the ring.

It is. But I walked it proudly, my head held high. I climbed into the ring, saluted my supporters and flung off my dressing-gown. And the crowd went wild!

Why?

I'd forgotten to put my shorts on.

What was your opponent like?

He was pretty mean looking. And just before the fight started, my trainer yelled in my ear that my opponent beat his wife, kicked his kids and starved his mother. That sort of behaviour makes me fighting mad!

I'll bet!

I can't stand people shouting in my ear.

How did the fight go?

Well, for a minute or two I was in with a great chance. Then it started.

The bell went?

Yes. I raced out of my corner, tried a left, then another left, then a right!

Fantastic!

Then my opponent came out of his corner. But within a minute, I really had him worried.

Why?

He thought he'd killed me.

What happened?

I was flat on my back.

I bet you were mad.

I was livid! I was ready to jump up and belt him one! But then I thought I'd better count to ten before I did anything hasty.

Oh no! Didn't your trainer shout at you?

Yes, he was shouting, 'Laundry, Laundry! Get up!'

'Laundry?' Why did he call you 'Laundry'?

'Cos I was always hanging over the ropes.

And the crowd were yelling the same thing?

No – they were yelling, 'Rembrandt, Rembrandt! Get up!'

'Rembrandt?' Why 'Rembrandt'?

'Cos I was always on the canvas. Then my opponent spoke to me.

What did he say?

He said, 'Don't worry – I'm only going to hit you with one hand.'

Why?

He needed the other to hold me up. But I was still swinging away at him. Not actually hitting him, but it was my only chance.

How do you mean?

Well, I thought if I kept swinging, the draught might give him a cold.

Didn't your trainer have any advice?

Yes, he shouted at me to let him hit me with his right for a while.

Why?

My face had gone crooked. But it was too late. The next blow was the final one.

You were knocked out?

I was knocked out so much I almost had to pay to get back in again. Still, I reckon I could have got up off the canvas and fought on if it hadn't been for the ref.

Why, what was he doing?

He was standing on my hand.

Still, you did your best – that's the main thing.

Absolutely. I felt very proud. All right, I'd lost. But after the fight they presented me with a special cup.

To put on your mantelpiece?

No – to keep my teeth in.

23 · Court napping!

Order! Order in court!

Thank you, your honour. Mine's a pint of mild and bitter and a cheese sandwich.

Name?

Duncan, sir.

Duncan Who?

Duncan Disorderly.

Is this the first time you've been up before me?

I don't know – what time do you normally get up?

You are charged with assault, bigamy, dangerous driving ...

I don't recognise this court!

Why not?

You've had it decorated.

I must also charge you for burglary.

Fine – what do I owe you?

Do you plead guilty or not guilty?

I don't know – I haven't heard the evidence.

Have you ever been cross-examined before?

Yes, your honour, I'm married.

To how many wives?

Just the one, your honour. Honestly.

In that case I'll drop that charge. That's bigamy.

It's very big of you, your honour.

So if you're cleared on the other charges, too, you may go home.

Thank you, your honour – to which one?

Now then, the burglary charge. Why is it that every time you've been caught, you've been robbing a third floor flat?

Well, your honour, that's my storey and I'm sticking to it.

The charge is that you stole a petticoat.

Your honour, it was my first slip.

What have you got to say in your defence?

Well, your honour, my wife and I had been fighting that evening ...

Liquor, I suppose.

No, actually – she licked me this time.

But you were under the influence of drink.

You're right – I was drunk as a judge.

You mean: Drunk as a *Lord.*

Yes, my Lord.

So that would explain your driving offences. You were driving down a one-way street.

But I was only driving one way, your honour.

But didn't you see the arrows?

Arrows? I didn't even see the Indians!

Where were you going?

I can't remember. But everyone else seemed to be coming back.

I'm going to teach you that crime doesn't pay.

I know it doesn't – but the hours are good.

Of the driving offences I find you guilty. Thirty days or £250.

I'll take the £250.

Of the charge of robbery, I find you innocent.

Thank you, your honour. Just one question.

What's that?

Does that mean I can keep the loot?

24 · Not tonight Josephine!

Good evening, ladies and gentlemen. My name is Colonel Napoleon Davenport DSO, MC, OBE.

That's a funny way to spell Davenport.

Are you maligning my decorations?

I never touched them!

To continue: and I'm here tonight to tell you about my most famous ancestor, after whom I, Napoleon Davenport, am named.

No!

Yes.

You're descended from . . .

That's right.

. . . Wilf Davenport, the legendary Stockport County centre forward! This is fantastic! Let me shake your hand!

You ignorant fool! I'm talking about Napoleon Bonaparte, Emperor of France. A brave fighter!

Absolutely!

He was nothing if not a brilliant soldier.

In other words he was nothing.

Do you mind!

Sorry – no offence. Actually, I've nothing but admiration for Napoleon.

Thank you.

And I've very little of that.

To continue: I have a painting of Napoleon at home. He's mounted on horseback and he's cutting a fine figure.

He's sitting on his sword!

Napoleon rode that horse all over Europe. He rode from Paris to Italy, from Italy to Paris, from Paris to Austria, from Austria to Paris, from Paris to Russia, from Russia to Paris. And do you know why he kept riding back to Paris?

He kept forgetting his saddle?

No. He'd decided the time had come to take a wife.

And the question was, whose wife to take?

And he had met Josephine – a woman of whom it would be said today that she really had something that would knock your eye out.

A husband.

In fact, her marriage was over by the time she met Napoleon. And she fell immediately, madly in love with him.

Despite the fact that he was only four foot six inches tall. He used to take shelter from the rain standing under his horse.

Do you mind! Napoleon Bonaparte did in fact stand five feet in his socks.

Five feet in his socks? Most people have only two feet in them!

But Josephine did not mind his relative lack of stature. Her attitude was ...

Better to have loved a short man than never to have loved a tall.

You are a very foolhardy man to insult the honour of the Napoleon family.

Lot of sissies.

What do you mean? Every Napoleon since Bonaparte himself has been buried with full military honours!

No!

And do you know what a man must be to be buried with full military honours?

Yes I do.

What?

Dead.

25 · Like no business we know!

Hello! Long time no see. How are you?

Fine, thanks.

Got a job yet?

Got a terrific job.

Great! What are you doing?

I work in the circus – mucking out the elephants.

Mucking out the elephants? How many are there of them?

Twenty-five.

Twenty-five elephants! How much do they pay you?

Seven pounds fifty pence a week.

Seven pounds fifty a week for mucking out twenty-five elephants! That's terrible! If I were you, I'd chuck it all in and get an office job.

What, and give up show business?

Is there any chance of advancement?

There might be – they've just fired the human cannon-ball. And they're looking for someone of the same calibre.

Wait a minute – you were with the circus before. You were engaged to a lady contortionist. What happened?

She broke it off.

Very painful. You must have show business in your blood.

I have. When I was eight I ran away with a circus.

Really?

Yes. Then, when I was nine, they made me bring it back again. So after that I decided to go into the theatre. My father had given me a drum and told me to beat it.

But you were still a child! How did you support yourself?

I taught piano playing.

Taught piano playing?

Yes, I taught piano playing was easy – but I soon learned it was hard. So I started to practise on the sly – which is a lot more difficult than practising on the piano.

99

How long was it before you got a job in the theatre?

Not long. It wasn't half as difficult as people said it would be.

Can you remember the first words you spoke in the theatre.

I'll never forget them. How could I?

Tell me them.

'This way, please! Programmes! ...' After a couple of months came my big break. That great Shakespearian actor and dance band leader, Sir Lawrence Olivier, came to the theatre.

What happened?

He came up to me. My heart stopped. He said, 'Young man, have you read any of Shakespeare's plays?'

What did you say?

I said, 'Only two of them.' He said, 'Which ones?' I said, 'Romeo and Juliet.' So he put me in his next play.

What was it about?

It was about thirty minutes too long.

What was the audience like?

Well, on the first night, there was nobody there at all, but on the second the attendance fell off completely.

That's bad.

You call that bad. On the Saturday night, we sent the audience home in a taxi.

Did you suffer from stage fright?

I did, but I found a cure for it.

What's that?

You take a twenty minute walk three minutes before you go on. Actually it was nice to get out of that theatre – it was a real dump.

How come?

My dressing-room was so small, every time I stood up, I hit my head on the chain.

That's terrible.

Mind you, there was running water on every floor.

Well, that's not so bad.

Except that it made the dog-ends a bit soggy.

102

Was that the high point of your career in show business?

No, that was just the beginning. I became quite a well-known actor.

Really?

Yes. Did you, for instance, see my Bottom at Stratford-upon-Avon?

No.

A pity – many people consider it my best part. But, above all, I consider myself a film actor.

Really?

Oh, yes. For instance, did you see Star Wars?

Yes?

So did I. Terrific wasn't it?

26 · Look at the thighs of her!

What's all that green stuff in your bag?

Lettuce. Six heads of it. It's for the wife.

Is she on a diet?

Yes, she has six heads of lettuce a day. That's her limit. The doctor says if she has any more, he'll be treating her for greenfly.

Is she overweight, then?

Well, I'm not saying she's fat but we've been married six years and I still haven't seen all of her.

But you told me the other day she had a million dollar figure!

She has. Trouble is, it's all in loose change. When she goes in a phone box, half of her stays outside.

Was she fat when you first met her?

I'll say! She was sunbathing on the beach at Blackpool and a policeman came along. 'You'll have to move,' he said. 'The tide's waiting to come in.'

What did she weigh?

I asked her actually. She said, 'I tip the scales at eleven stone three pounds.' She didn't tip them.

No?

No – she bribed them. She had so many double chins, I thought at first I was looking at her over a stack of pancakes.

But she must have had an attractive nature.

Oh, she did. She was so gentle and sweet and obliging.

Aah!

Yes – she wouldn't hurt an elephant. And she used to go round all the time, singing away to herself.

How lovely.

The thing was, her mouth was so big, she could sing duets by herself.

It must have been quite a sight.

It was. But you should have seen her when she yawned.

What happened?

Her ears disappeared.

105

But none the less, you asked her to marry you.

Oh yes. Mind you, at the wedding, she needed three relatives to give her away. And when I carried her over the threshold, I had to make two trips.

Doesn't she get any exercise?

Only jumping to conclusions and running up bills.

And does she watch her food?

Not for long. Mind you, she's very particular about what she eats.

Really?

Oh yes – there has to be lots of it. It's no wonder when she sits on a stool, most of her sits on the floor.

What does she do about having a bath?

I just take her to the car wash.

What, with her dress on?

Sure. Which reminds me – we've got a bit of a problem at home.

What's that?

Well, she washed her night-dress yesterday and put it out on the line to dry.

Yes?

When I looked out of the window this morning, a family of gypsies had moved in.

27 · She dresses to kill - and cooks the same way!

Why don't you wash your face – I can see what you had for breakfast this morning.

Really? What did I have?

Bacon and eggs.

Wrong – that was yesterday *morning. My wife was doing the cooking this morning so I settled for cornflakes. It's the only thing she can do.*

You must get sick of them.

I do. I've had so much cornflakes since I got married, I go soggy in the bath.

Did you have to teach her how to prepare cornflakes?

I did. When we first got married she used to spoil them every time.

How?

She used to boil them in the bag.

Did she know anything about cooking?

Not a thing. I'll never forget the first time she cooked for me. I can see her now, standing on her head in the kitchen, making an apple turnover.

Couldn't she even boil a pan of water?

Not without getting lumps in it. She couldn't even make ice-cubes.

Why not?

She couldn't find a recipe.

So she did have a recipe book?

Yes. It was published by the Dripping Marketing Board – Learn To Cook In Ten Greasy Lessons. *She liked the section on cooked breakfasts best, so we came to an understanding.*

Which was?

I brought home the bacon and she burnt it. Then it was fried fish. Morning, noon and night.

Every day?

Every day. I had so much fish during that first year, I was breathing through my cheeks.

But that's all she could cook?

That and her three-foot-long rhubarb tarts.

Three-foot-long rhubarb tarts?

Yes, that was the shortest rhubarb she could find. I remember one day she asked the butcher for a humpbacked rabbit.

Why?

So she could keep the piecrust up in the middle.

Are things much different now?

Oh yes – I now know what it means to go home at night to a three-course slap-up supper.

Really?

It means I've gone home to the wrong house, that's what it means. But I must be fair – I get a lump in my throat when I think of my wife's rock cakes.

How nice.

I get a lump in my throat when I eat my wife's rock cakes.

Does she still cook them?

Yes, she gave me a plateful last week. She said, 'Take your pick.' I didn't need a pick, I needed a hammer and chisel.

What on earth does she put in them?

That's the trouble – she only believes in using the right ingredients. Real rocks in the rock cakes. Her date loaf tastes like she put a whole diary into it. And her pastry!

What about it?

Well, I'm not saying it's heavy, but we're the only people in the street with a bow-legged gas stove.

At least she still perseveres.

Oh yes, she really likes being in the kitchen. Really she cooks for fun.

How nice.

Mind you, for meals we go out to a restaurant.

28 · I call my mother-in-law 'Echo' because she always has the last word!

Hey, let me buy you a drink. We've just had a blessed event at our house.

Really?

Yes, my mother-in-law's gone home.

How long was she with you?

Since last Sunday.

Last Sunday? Wasn't that the day I saw you digging that enormous hole in your front garden?

Yes, my wife said her mother was in the district and I was hoping she'd drop in.

But why did you fill it with water?

I wanted to drown my troubles.

Why, don't you get on with her?

Oh, it's not too bad. Apart from the fact that I beat her up every morning.

You don't.

I do – I get up at seven and she gets up at eight. Then I always take her morning tea in my pyjamas. But is she grateful?

No?

No – she says she'd rather have it in a cup. It's no wonder we're always arguing.

Really? Who wins?

Well, usually we agree to meet each other half-way.

How's that?

Well, she'll admit she's right if I'll admit I'm wrong. Trouble is, every now and again I do something that really hurts her.

Like what?

Like breathing. Mind you, I haven't spoken to her for four days.

Why's that?

I didn't like to interrupt her.

She talks a lot then?

I'll say. We spent yesterday on the beach. When we got her home, her tongue was sunburned.

And is she outspoken?

Not by many. Mind you, she's developed a slight impediment in her speech lately.

What's that?

She stops to breathe. It's a real strain, taking her everywhere.

But you don't have to take her everywhere.

I know – it's just that I hate having to kiss her goodbye. We took her shopping this morning. She's clothes mad.

Did she buy anything?

Yes, she bought a camel coat. When she put it on, you'd think the camel was still in it.

Was it expensive?

She *didn't think so. In fact she told me she thought she'd bought it for a ridiculous price. In fact she bought it for an absurd figure.*

Why, what does she look like?

Walking down the street, she looks like two small boys fighting under a blanket. She said to me, 'Don't you think I'd look terrific in something flowing?' I said, 'Yes, try the River Thames.'

Was she insulted?

I'll say. She went on and on about it.

And did you give her as good as you got?

Of course – I gave her a really good listening to. But if you saw her you'd know what I mean.

Can you remember the first time you saw her?

I'll never forget it – don't think I haven't tried. She'd just been in for a face lift. But they couldn't do it. So for seventy-five quid they lowered her body. You must meet her one day.

Well, I don't know ...

No, you must. Then you'll know why I drink.

Can't you think of anything good to say about her?

Well, I will say this; there was once a time when I think I would have cut my throat if it wasn't for my mother-in-law.

How d'you mean?

She was using my razor.

29 ·Party lines!

Hello! Welcome to the party!

I don't want to come to the party. I live downstairs and I've come up to complain about the row! I'm looking for the people who live here.

Well, you've certainly come to the right place.

Didn't you hear me pounding on the ceiling?

Oh, that's OK – we were making a lot of noise ourselves. We're celebrating his grandad's one hundred and third birthday.

Really?

Yes. Pity his grandad can't be here though.

Why's that?

He died ten years ago. Still, it's not bad for a Gay Nineties Party.

A Gay Nineties Party? How d'you mean?

Well, all the men are gay and all the women are ninety. Do you drink?

No.

Then hold this bottle while I tie my shoelaces.

Don't you think you've had enough to drink?

What! Look, I may be very slightly under the affluence of incohol but I'm certainly not as think as you drunk I am. Certaily not.

Well, you look as if you've had too much to me.

See those stairs, there?

Yes.

Well, I just fell down them with two pints of whisky.

Did you spill any?

No, I kept my mouth closed. Anyway, now you're up here, why don't you join us in a game of Cowboy's Knock?

Cowboy's Knock? What's that?

It's the same as Postman's Knock but there's more horsin' around.

No thanks, I don't think I will.

Well, why don't you have a dance?

Actually, I don't think I will – I'm a little stiff from badminton.

It doesn't matter where you're from – you can still join in. Why don't you go in for the spot dance?

Why?

Well, with a complexion like yours, you're bound to win. Tell you what, though. Why don't you stay and play this terrific game we've invented?

How do you play it?

Well, ten of us go into a room and sit down on the floor and we drink three bottles of scotch each and then one of us goes outside.

Yes?

And the rest of us have to guess who it is.

You're *so* drunk.

Really? So am I. Still, you've got all day Sober to sunday up in.

No, I'm talking about *you.*

Me? No, I'm not as drunk as some thinkle peep I am. See that terrific blonde over there?

Yes?

She's been annoying me all evening.

I bet she hasn't even looked at you.

I know – that's what keeps annoying me.

I can't talk to you any more. You're just too drunk.

Drunk? I've had at most tee martoonies.

I'm going anyway.

Look, tell you what: Why don't you come round to my *place next Saturday?*

Why what's happening?

I'm having a Coming Out party for my sister.

Really?

Yes – she's just done six months in Holloway.

'What do you think of it so far?'

30 · Endpiece

A Personal Message from Eric and Ernie to You!

Hey _____! Do you want to be world
<u>WRITE YOUR NAME HERE</u>

famous in _____? Would you like to be one
<u>YOUR TOWN HERE</u>

of _____'s best loved comedians?
<u>YOUR ROAD OR STREET HERE</u>

_____ Well, now, with the aid of *The Morecambe and*
<u>WRITE YES HERE</u>

Wise Jokebook, it's easy! You've got the scripts here. Now,

all you need is a partner. Ask your brother, or sister, or

Mum, or Dad – even Auntie _____.
<u>YOUR AUNTIE'S NAME HERE</u>

Toss up to decide which of you delivers the feed lines and

which the punch lines, find yourself an audience and away

you go.

And remember, you're going out there a _____
<u>YOUR JOB HERE</u>

– and you're coming back a star!

Good Luck!

ERIC AND ERNIE